Aboriginal Legends of Canada

Iroquois

Megan Cuthbert

Weigl

Published by Weigl Educational Publishers Limited
6325 10th Street SE
Calgary, Alberta T2H 2Z9

Website: www.weigl.ca

Library and Archives Canada Cataloguing in Publication available upon request.
Fax 403-233-7769 for the Publishing Records Department.

ISBN 978-1-77071-557-8 (hardcover)
ISBN 978-1-77071-558-5 (softcover)
ISBN 978-1-77071-559-2 (multi-user ebook)

Printed in the United States of America in North Mankato, Minnesota
1 2 3 4 5 6 7 8 9 0 17 16 15 14 13

072013
WEP130613

Project Coordinator: Heather Kissock
Editor: Alexis Roumanis
Art Director: Mandy Christiansen
Illustrator: Martha Jablonski-Jones

Photo Credits
Weigl acknowledges Alamy and Getty Images as its primary image suppliers for this title.

We acknowledge the financial support of the Government of Canada through the Canada Book Fund for our publishing activities.

CONTENTS

4   Meet the Iroquois

6   Stories of Creation

8   The Story of Sky Mother

10 Nature Stories

12 How the Chipmunk
    Got its Stripes

14 Life Lessons

16 Why Crows Are Poor

18 Heroic Tales

20 The Story of Hiawatha

22 Activity

23 Further Research

24 Key Words/Index

Meet the Iroquois

Hundreds of years ago, five North American **Aboriginal** groups came together to create one of the world's first **democracies**. This was known as the Iroquois Confederacy. Today, the confederacy is made up of the Mohawk, Oneida, Onondaga, Cayuga, Seneca, and Tuscarora people. They live mainly in southern Ontario and Quebec, as well as parts of the northern United States.

Each group in the Iroquois Confederacy has its own **culture**, land, and **traditions.** One of the traditions is storytelling. Families often gather to hear **elders** tell stories. Some stories explain the history of the Iroquois Confederacy. Others are about the creation of the **natural world**. Many stories demonstrate the difference between good and bad behaviour.

Stories of Creation

The Iroquois use storytelling to explain how the world came to be. These creation stories introduce children and others to Iroquois beliefs. Most Iroquois believe in a powerful creator named the Great Spirit. They believe that the Great Spirit is responsible for all living things.

Before Earth was formed, the Great Spirit ruled over the Sky World. In the middle of Sky World stood the Tree of Life. The Great Spirit had warned people not to harm the tree. When Sky Woman disobeyed this order, a new world was formed.

The Iroquois often gathered to celebrate and give thanks for the gifts of the Great Spirit. Ceremonies honoured different harvests and events throughout the year.

The Tree of Life is often described as a maple tree.

Women have long played an important role in Iroquois society. In the past, they were responsible for taking care of the children, making clothing, and preparing food for their families.

The Story of SKY MOTHER

In the beginning, there was a water world inhabited by animals that could live without land. Above them was a Sky World, which was inhabited by human-like beings, plants, and animals.

The Tree of Life grew in the middle of Sky World. The tree was important to the creatures of Sky World because it was the entrance to the world below. One day, Sky Woman became curious and asked her brother to uproot the tree. Beneath the tree was a large hole. Sky Woman leaned over to peer into the hole. As she looked, she slipped and began falling into the world below.

Birds heard Sky Woman's cry for help. They flew to her and cushioned her fall. They then placed her on the back of a giant turtle. The water creatures were worried that Sky Woman would not survive without land, so they each took turns diving to the bottom of the ocean to grab dirt. Dirt was placed on the back of the turtle. The pile of dirt grew until it became what is now known as North America.

Nature Stories

The natural world is very important to the Iroquois, since much of their survival depends on it. The Iroquois have several stories, or **legends**, that explain how the natural world works. Some of these stories explain the different appearances or behaviour of animals. The stories are a fun and entertaining way for Iroquois children to learn about the world around them.

How the Chipmunk Got Its Stripes explains how the chipmunk came to have black stripes running along its back. In doing so, it highlights some of the traits specific animals have. Chipmunks are small and clever. Bears are strong and confident.

To the Iroquois, the bear represents strength and power.

Chipmunks are featured in only a few Aboriginal stories.

How the CHIPMUNK Got its STRIPES

Bear was very confident because he was so big and strong. He believed there was nothing he could not do. Chipmunk was tired of the Bear's boasting. He believed he was smarter than Bear and wanted to prove it. "If you can do anything, why don't you see if you can stop the Sun from rising?" he challenged Bear.

Bear believed he could do anything, so he agreed to the challenge. He turned so that he was facing the east and willed the Sun not to rise. It did not work. The Sun rose like it always did. This made Chipmunk very happy. He ran around Bear, laughing and gloating. Bear became very angry. He grabbed Chipmunk and pinned him to the ground. Sensing the danger, Chipmunk tried to calm Bear, complimenting him on how big and strong he was. Bear was having none of it. He refused to loosen his grip on Chipmunk. Luckily, Chipmunk managed to squirm free from Bear's paw. As he ran away, Bear tried to grab him. His claws scraped down Chipmunk's back as Chipmunk ran away. This is why, even today, chipmunks have stripes on their backs.

Life Lessons

The Iroquois use stories to teach important lessons to their children. These stories often feature animals or funny characters that are faced with a problem. The actions they take can lead to either a solution or more problems. These stories encourage children to think about the consequences of their actions.

Storytelling is only one way the Iroquois pass on their legends. Iroquois legends are also told through art, music, and dance.

Why Crows Are Poor teaches an important lesson about planning for hard times. The Iroquois were both hunters and farmers. As such, crops were very important to their survival. The Iroquois had to plan when to plant and harvest their crops, and to make sure they had enough food for the long winter. The story explains why planning is important and why it is necessary to be prepared.

Corn, beans, and squash were staples in the Iroquois diet. The Iroquois called these foods the Three Sisters. They were planted and eaten together.

Harvest was an important time for the Iroquois. They had to bring in their crops before the cold weather arrived, or they would not have enough food to survive the winter.

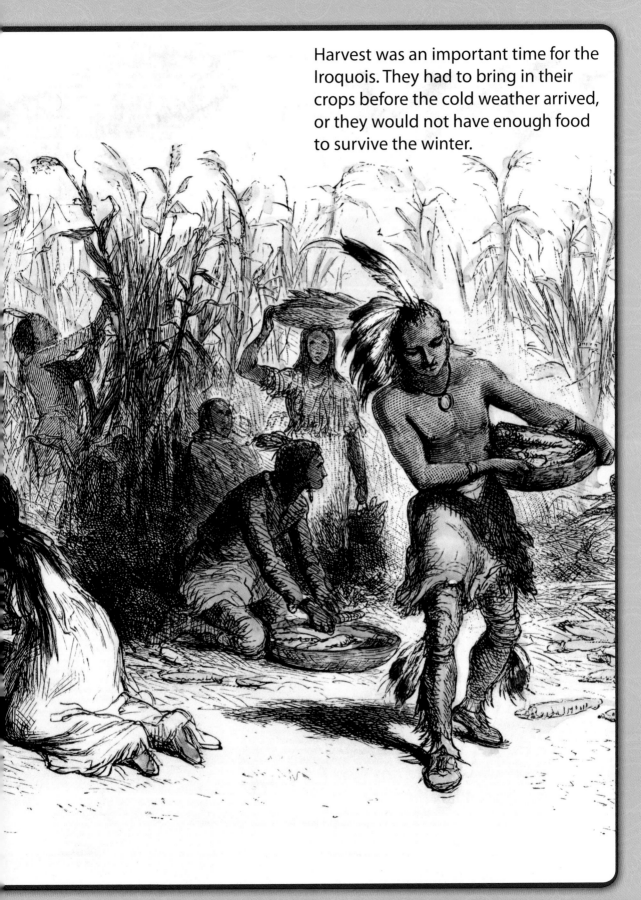

Why CROWS Are POOR

When the Great Spirit gave the people the gift of corn, the crow claimed that he had been the one asked to bring the corn to them. Because of his good deed, the crow believed that he and his friends had the right to take the corn when it was ready for harvest. The crows were not greedy, however, and only took what they needed, never more. In the summer, they happily took the corn they needed to feed themselves. When summer became winter, there was no more corn, and the crows became sad and hungry.

The crows decided that next summer, they would take more corn and store it. This way, they would not be hungry in the winter. They all agreed that it was a very good plan.

When summer came, the crows were too happy to think about the coming winter. They forgot their plan and took only the corn they needed for the moment. When winter finally came, the crows were hungry once again.

Heroic Tales

Some Iroquois stories are based on real people. These people have acted in heroic ways and have helped the Iroquois through their actions. In these stories or legends, the heroes use their skills to overcome obstacles. They set an example for others to follow.

One of the Iroquois's greatest heroes was a chief called Hiawatha. He was one of the leaders responsible for forming the Iroquois Confederacy. Although not everyone thought it would be a good idea to unite the different groups, Hiawatha was able to convince the people that the confederacy would make the groups stronger. Eventually, he was able to bring the people together. Over time, the story has changed, but it still preserves an important part of Iroquois history.

It is believed that, when the confederacy first formed, the leaders tied five arrows together, one from each of the original member groups. Since then, a bundle of five arrows has come to symbolize the unity of the Iroqouis Confederacy.

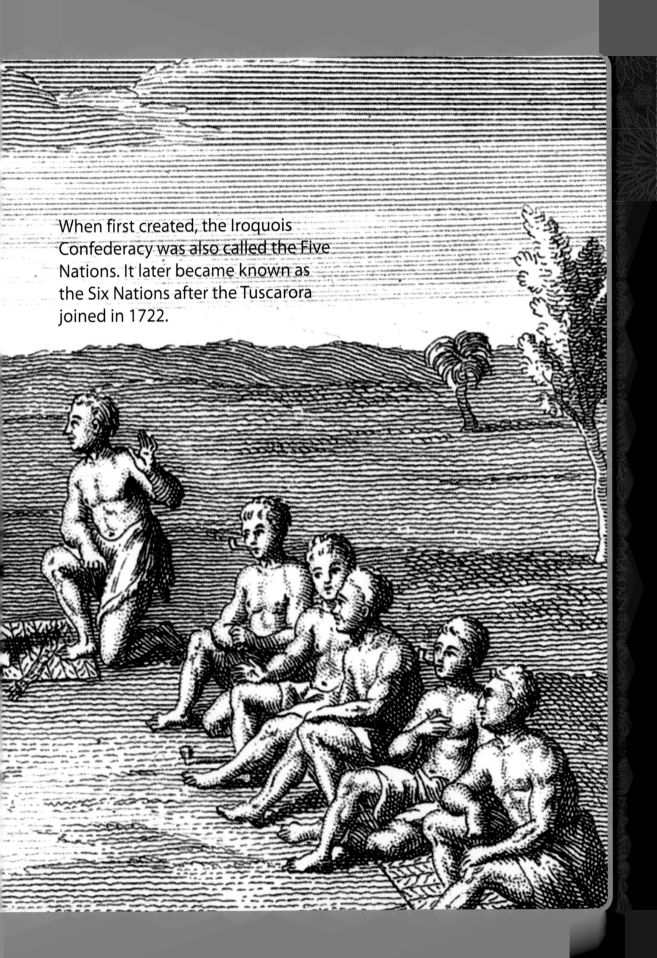

When first created, the Iroquois Confederacy was also called the Five Nations. It later became known as the Six Nations after the Tuscarora joined in 1722.

The Story of HIAWATHA

Hiawatha was a member of the Mohawk tribe. When he became chief, he met a **prophet** named Dekanawida, who believed the people of the Mohawk, Oneida, Onondaga, Cayuga, and Seneca nations should unite. Hiawatha believed in Dekanawida's plan, and went out to explain the plan to the other **First Nations**.

The powerful Onondaga chief, Atotarho, did not like Hiawatha's plan. He sent a giant white bird to take Hiawatha's daughter and kill her. Despite the loss of his daughter, Hiawatha continued with his plan. He travelled to the different villages on his magical white canoe, trying to convince the people to join together.

Finally, the people agreed to Hiawatha's plan. He gave each group a different role in protecting the new nation, and he named them the Iroquois. Having finished his task, he sailed into the air in his magical canoe.

Activity

Build a Longhouse

The Iroquois call themselves the Haudenosaunee, which means People of the Longhouse. An Iroquois longhouse was made with wood frames and covered with bark. It could be up to 30 metres long. Follow these steps to make a smaller version of an Iroquois longhouse.

You Will Need:

bark   scissors   glue   an empty box

1. Turn the empty box upside down.

2. With an adult's help, use the scissors to cut a doorway at both ends of the box.

3. Glue bark onto the box until it is covered. Put your longhouse on display for others to see.

Further Research

Many books and websites provide information on Aboriginal legends. To learn more about this topic, borrow books from the library, or search the internet.

Books

Most libraries have computers that connect to a database for researching information. If you input a key word, you will be provided with a list of books in the library that contain information on that topic. Nonfiction books are arranged numerically, using their call number. Fiction books are organized alphabetically by the author's last name.

Websites

Learn more about the Iroquois at: www.everyculture.com/multi/Ha-La/Iroquois-Confederacy

To hear more Iroquois legends, visit : www.tuscaroras.com/index. php/stories-and-legends

Key Words

Aboriginal: First Nations, Inuit, and Métis of Canada

culture: the arts, beliefs, and habits of a community, people, or country

democracies: governments in which decisions are made by the people or their chosen representatives

elders: the wise people of a community

First Nations: members of Canada's Aboriginal community who are not Inuit or Métis

legends: stories that have been passed down from generation to generation

natural world: relating to things that have not been made by people

prophet: someone who speaks for a god

traditions: established practices and beliefs

Index

corn 6, 14, 16

Great Spirit 6, 16

Hiawatha 18, 20, 21

Iroquois Confederacy 4, 18, 19